THE Artist IN you

Julie Brunelle
and
Peter Wood

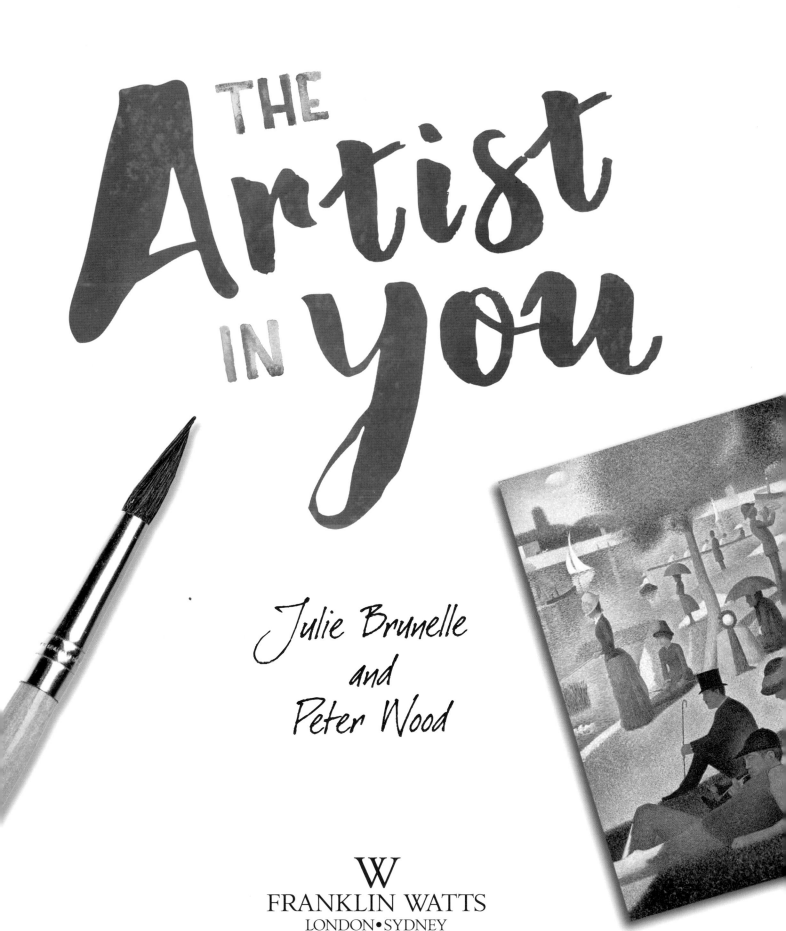

W

FRANKLIN WATTS
LONDON • SYDNEY

This book is dedicated to our favourite students, our niece and nephew, Adelyn and Oliver, to Peter's teacher, Gerald Ferguson and finally to Julie's mentor, Ms Daniela Parkinson. May this book be our quid pro quo for the delight and satisfaction we find in art.

Franklin Watts

First published in Great Britain in 2017 by The Watts Publishing Group

Text copyright © Julie Brunelle and Peter Wood 2017

Step-by-step illustrations © Julie Brunelle and Peter Wood 2017

Editor: Sarah Peutrill
Designer: Jennifer Rose Design

Picture credits: See page 64

ISBN: 978 1 4451 5169 4

Printed in China

Franklin Watts
An imprint of
Hachette Children's Group
Part of The Watts Publishing Group

Carmelite House
50 Victoria Embankment
London EC4Y 0DZ

An Hachette UK Company

www.hachette.co.uk

www.franklinwatts.co.uk

CONTENTS

"EVERYTHING STARTS FROM A DOT."

Wassily Kandinsky

The start part

THE TOOLS OF AN ARTIST

To complete any artwork, artists use countless tools. Some of them are physical tools, such as paintbrushes, pencils and paint. Some tools are techniques and skills. Others are more subtle, such as the elements and principles of art and design, which are just as important in creating a successful piece of art.

Like any other discipline, art has its own language or specialised vocabulary used to talk about works of art and how they were created. Have you ever gone to a museum and your companion asks, 'What do you think?' You are not sure what to say: you know it's nice and that you like it, but you are not sure how to express your views. This book is here to help you learn to express yourself about art.

THE ELEMENTS OF ART

The basis of art language is the elements of art. There are between five and ten elements, depending on who you ask. However, most people agree that there are seven key elements. This book investigates the element of point as well as the other more common art elements: line, shape, texture, form, tone, space and colour. Although these elements are explored separately to give you a deeper understanding of each, they do not work independently. They work together to enhance one another, and also to create certain visual effects.

SO, WHAT IS THIS BOOK ABOUT?

This book has two objectives. One is to introduce the basics of art and the art-making process in an easy, accessible way with fun projects, while exploring various mediums* and techniques. The second is to introduce you to the language of art so that you can begin using art terms to discuss works of art.

SO LET'S GET TO THE POINT ...

* Not sure what we mean by 'medium'? Go to the glossary on page 60 to find out. There are lots of technical terms in this book but each one is explained in the glossary so don't forget to check there when you need to. There is also a section on art movements on pages 58–59 and tips for perfecting some art techniques on pages 54–57.

POINT

Point is a good place to start when creating a work of art. When a person lays a pencil or paintbrush on a surface, the dot is created. It is full of potential. From that point, it can become anything. If you move that point, a line is created, which can become a shape, a form and then anything you can imagine.

WHAT THE VIEWER SEES

Even by laying just one point on a page, the viewer begins to make relationships to it by considering its location, size, colour and form. When there are two dots, the viewer begins to make connections and establishes an invisible 'line' linking the two points. If there are three points, the viewer will 'see' a triangle. Artists use these ideas to lead the viewer's eye around an artwork.

Roy Lichtenstein (1923–1997) uses Ben-Day dots to produce half-tones in *Girl with Hair Ribbon* (1965).

Georges Seurat layers dots of paint to produce a vibrating effect in his famous painting *A Sunday Afternoon on the Island of La Grande Jatte* (detail) (1884) – see page 11.

Points can be used to create tone and colour in a drawing or painting. To give a shape the illusion of form, some artists will build up an object using small dots. When the points are close together a dark tone is created; place the dots further apart and a lighter tone will emerge. Points can be used as part of an implied line, such as a dotted line. These techniques are used primarily in drawing, pen and ink and printmaking.

Yayoi Kusama (1929–), also known as the 'polka dot princess', uses repeating dot patterns in new and creative ways to create breathtaking, large-scale sculptures and installations, such as *Yellow Pumpkin* (1994–2004).

VISUAL EFFECTS

Artists often use points to create interesting visual effects. The pointillist artists, Georges Seurat (1859–1891) and Camille Pissarro (1830–1903), overlaid dots of colour to create the effect of flickering light in their paintings. Lichtenstein used Ben-Day dots (see page 8) in his work to create the illusion of half-tones. Points can also be used as part of a pattern, such as the well-known polka dot design, which consists of a series of little round circles placed in a varying grid-like format. Artist Yayoi Kusama (above) creates fantastical effects by covering entire rooms with polka dots. Lastly, by varying size, direction and colour, points or dots can be used to create decorative designs that cover our everyday objects, such as books, cloth, wallpaper and carpets.

THE Lichtenstein SELFIE

Roy Lichtenstein was an important artist in the American pop art movement. He painted large scale works based on the style of printed comic-book illustrations.

Like comic books, Lichtenstein used Ben-Day dots to create any colour that was a tint. Ben-Day dots are little circles of colour placed next to each other to create an illusion of another colour or half-tone. In *Masterpiece*, notice how Lichtenstein uses solid primary colours (red, yellow and blue) and black and white, but also includes red Ben-Day dots for the pink skin colour. Keep this in mind when designing your painting.

Masterpiece (1962)

- In which parts of the painting can you see Ben-Day dots?

- What can you see in the background? The overall colour is blue and there seems to be a window or the shadow of a window.

- Look at the text. The speech is very dramatic and notice the variation in the font size and width.

- One figure is turning towards the viewer and the other is in side profile. Try using one of these views to create a dramatic composition.

TIP!

Skin tones

Creating skin tones can be challenging. For darker skin tones, begin by mixing white paint with a little brown. Brown is a strong colour so you will only need a touch of brown in the white. Some skin tones have a yellow undertone, and others a pink undertone. Try adding a little yellow or red. Remember that acrylic paint dries darker, so test your colours first.

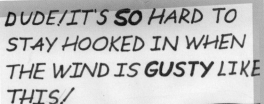

You will need

- a smartphone with a camera
- a computer and printer
- sheets of A4 paper
- masking tape
- thin white card
- a pencil
- a black marker pen
- acrylic paints
- a small flat paintbrush
- toothpicks (or a very fine paintbrush)

1 Take a series of selfies with fun expressions and interesting props, such as your favourite hat. Choose the best one. Print it in black and white on A4 paper.

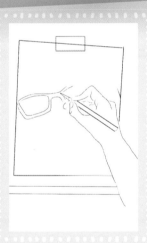

2 Tape the selfie print onto a window (see page 56) and use another piece of tape to fix the card on top of it. Leave space for the speech bubble. Trace the main features with a pencil. It's important to minimise lines around the nose. Go over the lines with a marker pen.

3 Consider your design and colour scheme. Ask yourself: will I include any objects in the background? What areas will be blocked in with primary colours, and what areas will be covered with Ben-Day dots? Draw in your background objects.

4 Begin by carefully painting your primary colours with a nice even layer of paint using the small flat brush. Next, paint your Ben-Day dots using a toothpick (or very thin paintbrush). Take care to paint one dot at a time.

5 On a computer, type in the text for the speech bubble using the Comic Sans font in caps and italic. Print it. You may have to make some adjustments to make it fit. Using the same transfer technique as in step 2, trace the text on your card, and go over the letters with a marker pen.

Seurat's DOTTED LANDSCAPE

A pointillist artist named Georges Seurat was wild about dots. He loved dots so much that he created entire paintings made up of painted dots.

This painting technique is called pointillism, where an artist uses dots of pure colour placed close to each other. The dots blend together when viewed from a distance. One of Seurat's most famous paintings is *A Sunday Afternoon on the Island of La Grande Jatte*.

- What objects can you see? There are dogs, a monkey, parasols and much more.

- Look at the colour scheme. It mainly consists of different shades and tints of green, blue and red. Red and green are complementary colours (see page 48).

You will need
- a sketchbook
- a sheet of A4 thick white card
- watercolour pencils
- a 2H pencil
- a cup of water
- paper towels

MAKE AN EXPRESSIONIST POINTILLIST PAINTING

1 Choose three or four subjects from Seurat's painting for your painting. Practise drawing them a few times in your sketchbook.

2 Begin by drawing the basic background composition. Lightly sketch the horizon line, the lines that create the water's edge and some trees.

3 Using light pencil lines, copy the three or four subjects from Seurat's painting. Notice that the subjects in the foreground are the largest, and the subjects in the background are the smallest.

A Sunday Afternoon on the Island of La Grande Jatte, 1884

4 Choose your colour scheme and prepare your paints. Test out your colours on a separate piece of card. Planning out your colour scheme will help you create mood and draw the viewer's eye around your work.

TIP!

Make one or two thumbnail sketches to work out your composition. Consider your focal point, which is the centre of interest. Move the subjects around until you achieve a balanced composition.

Try using harmonious colours – colours next to each other on the colour wheel (see page 48). Consider using a complementary colour for the focal point. Also, you may want to experiment with the watercolour pencils first.

Colour mixing

Adding white or black is not always the best way to make a colour lighter or darker. Instead, try using the colours from the colour wheel next to the colour you are trying to change. For example, to make a lighter shade of red, try adding some orange; to make a darker shade of red, try adding some purple. See pages 48–49 for more on the colour wheel.

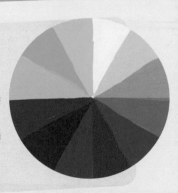

5 Dip your pencil into the cup of water. Begin by filling in the background with the watercolour pencils, one dot at a time.

6 Carefully paint all the subjects. Start with the lightest tones. Next layer the medium and darker tones. Remember, the white comes from the white of the paper.

LINE

As simple as it may appear, a line serves many functions in art. An artist uses lines not only to interpret objects in an artwork, but also to convey mood, expression and movement. Line is often used as a compositional tool to structure an artwork. Artists know that our eyes will naturally seek out lines and will follow the direction of a line. We can use this knowledge to create effects and to lead the viewer's eye around a composition.

WHAT IS A LINE?

A line is the path left by a moving point. There are many different types of line; they are one-dimensional and measured by length. The four main types of line are: vertical, horizontal, diagonal and curved. All other lines are variations of these four. From these, artists can vary the thickness, the direction, the location, the length and the degree of curve to create a variety of different effects.

Henry Moore (1898–1986) applies pencil, ink, gouache paint and wax to create his expressive lines in *Pink and Green Sleepers* (1941).

Lee Krasner (1908–1984) uses bold, curved and straight lines to express feelings of grief in her painting *Gothic Landscape* (1961).

MAKING LINES

If you look closely at the world around you, a line does not exist in the natural world. Lines are how humans transfer what we see onto paper, stone, wood etc. What we see are forms and to draw these forms, we interpret their edges. Together the edge of the form and its background creates the illusion, an outline of the object. An artist uses contour lines to simplify the shapes. He or she can create form using hatch lines and cross-hatch lines to give the illusion of three dimensions to an object.

Edvard Munch (1863–1944) uses many lines to direct our eyes around his painting in *The Scream* (1893).

CHANGING FEELINGS

Depending on the type of line and the medium and/or tool used to create the line, its quality or 'feeling' will vary. Curved lines can be expressive and promote feelings of excitement and aliveness, while straight lines promote feelings of consistency and monotony. The direction of the line also influences its quality. Horizontal lines can suggest calmness and restfulness; vertical lines can add height and spirituality, while diagonal lines can suggest movement or direction in an artwork.

PRINTING LINES
WITH
Klee

Paul Klee (1879–1940) was an expressionist artist who loved experimenting with colours and different types of line. Klee once said, 'Drawing is taking a line for a walk'.

Sometimes he would use unusual tools to create new and interesting lines. Take a look at Klee's famous painting, *Rising Sun*. It is a representation of a landscape.

MAKE AN EXPRESSIONIST
LANDSCAPE
PICTURE

You will need
- a 15 x 15 cm sheet of thick card
- a pencil
- black acrylic paint
- watercolour paints or watered down acrylic paints
- 'found' objects (whatever you think might make interesting lines, such as a paper cup, a feather or folded card)

When you can't think what to draw, a great way to get inspiration is to look at paintings by great artists, many of whom painted beautiful landscapes. Take a look at the works of Claude Monet (1840–1926), Winslow Homer (1836–1910) and Pieter Bruegel the Elder (1525–1569).

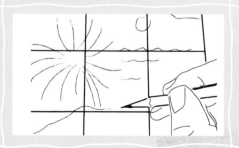

1 Plan the composition. Draw a few thumbnail sketches to experiment with your layout. Try using the rule of thirds (see page 57).

2 Begin your picture by lightly sketching your composition onto the card.

Rising Sun (1907)

- Repetition of line is an important part of this work. It creates a rhythm and unity. Can you describe the quality of the lines? Some are curved, straight, circular, long, rough or broken.

- Notice where Klee placed the focal point, the sun. He used the rule of thirds (see page 57) to structure this composition.

- Klee chose to use one main colour: yellow. He then used tints and shades of the other colours in the colour wheel (see pages 11, 48 and 49).

3 Experiment: dip the edge of one of your found objects in black paint and 'stamp' it onto paper to see what marks you can create. You may have to adjust the quantity of paint you are using or modify your object, such as cutting a paper cup.

4 Begin your artwork. Dip the edge of your object into black paint and begin creating marks on the thick card. When you have finished, wait for your black paint to dry.

5 Choose one dominant colour, as Klee did. Fill in the negative space (see page 42) with watered-down colours. (See page 55 for tips on watercolour painting.) Add the other colours here and there; try using each colour in three different parts of the painting to create balance. Let it dry. You may want to reapply some colours to certain areas to make the colours more intense.

TIP!

When painting with many different colours, the overall effect can be overwhelming, creating an artwork that is unbalanced. Paul Klee was a master of colour. It may be wise to limit your palette to three to four colours, until you become a master too.

LIGHT DRAWING WITH *Picasso*

Pablo Picasso (1881–1973) was an artist who loved to experiment. When photographer Gjon Mili (1904–1984) visited Picasso in his studio in 1949, the artists experimented with a photographic technique called light drawing. During this visit, Picasso created a photographic series displaying his iconic style using light and line, which can be seen in this artwork, entitled *Running Man*.

This type of drawing is described as gestural, which is a form of expressive mark making that captures the energy of a subject. Notice how Picasso creates a sense of rhythm and movement with his use of long, continuous and wavy lines.

Although we are surrounded by different lines, such as skylines, road lines and building lines, how an artist interprets line is unique. Just as we all have different signatures, each artist possesses his or her own line quality. Some artists use more curved lines, while others prefer to use hard, hatching lines in their work. The lines that an artist uses greatly influence the overall feelings created by the work.

Running Man (1949)

- Can you see the 'running man'? The head, two arms and two legs. Picasso used curved, circular, jagged and continuous lines to create the figure.

- How many images of Picasso can you see in the photo? This effect is created when the camera shutter is open for longer.

MAKE A
LIGHT DRAWING

You will need
- a camera that allows you to adjust the shutter speed
- a light source, such as a pointer or small bright torch
- a tripod or sturdy table
- a friend or two!

Setup Choose a room that you can make VERY dark. Set up your tripod or table about 2 m away from your friend. Adjust the camera setting to Shutter Speed Priority. Begin by selecting a shutter speed time of two seconds.

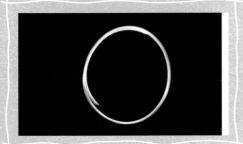

1 In the darkened room, ask your friend to make large circles with the torch or other light source. Take the photo and wait for the shutter to click. You'll need a few attempts to get this right.

2 Adjust the shutter speed to five seconds. Ask your friend to draw different lines and shapes with the light.

3 Adjust the shutter speed to ten seconds and ask your friend to try writing a word. Remember that he or she will have to write backwards and the letters will be backwards too. If you want to create spaces between the letters, your friend should hold a hand in front of the light while switching letters.

4 Adjust the shutter speed again to 15 seconds. Ask your friend to trace the outline of his or her body with the light. Try including random objects like a guitar, a cup or a chair.

5 Finally, adjust the shutter speed to 20 to 25 seconds, and ask your friend to draw a running man like Picasso's. It'll take a number of attempts before you achieve a result that you are satisfied with. Experiment, and have fun!

Shutter speed
The longer the shutter is open, the lighter (the more exposed) your photo will be. This will vary depending on how dark your room is. Another tip is to make sure that your friend is in focus before taking the shot.

SHAPE

As we have seen, a point can become a line, and when lines enclose space, they become shapes. A shape is an element of art that is two dimensional, therefore it is flat and is defined by its height and width. Shapes can be either geometric or irregular. Geometric shapes are created using mathematical laws of geometry, such as the circle, triangle and square. Irregular or organic shapes are those often found in nature. These irregular shapes can be composed of curved or angular lines, or a combination of the two.

THE BUILDING BLOCKS OF ART

A shape is often identified by its outline, but other times it is shaped by its bordering space because of variations in colour, texture or tone. Shapes are considered to be the building blocks of art. When artists reproduce an object, they will begin by breaking down complex forms, such as a horse or a flower, into an arrangement of basic shapes. Starting with these basic shapes, they will keep working on the artwork, adding details and texture. They may continue by using tone and colour to create a more accurate interpretation of the object.

Jean-Michel Basquiat (1960–1988) was known for using rough lines to create the shapes found in his work, such as *Untitled (Skull)* (1981).

In her painting *Prismes Electriques* (1914), Sonia Delaunay (1885–1979) uses both geometric and irregular shapes.

SHAPE AND FEELINGS

Each shape has is own 'personality'. Some will promote feelings of aggressiveness or stability in the viewer, while others will engender feelings of calm or otherworldliness. The quality of line used to construct a shape will also affect the qualities of the shape, thereby producing different feelings and associations. A shape created with a dark, rough line will promote a different feeling from one created with a smooth, gentle line.

COMPOSITION AND PATTERNS

Shapes are used in many different ways in making art. Not only can they interpret objects, but they can also be used in the composition of an artwork. The triangle was an important compositional tool in Renaissance art, used to represent stability and the Holy Trinity (God the Father, God the Son and God the Holy Spirit). Shapes are also an important part of pattern making and are used to decorate many of the flat surfaces around us, such as floors, walls, fabrics and books.

CUT-OUTS
WITH
Matisse

Amphitrite (1947)

MAKE A
CUT-OUT PICTURE

You will need
- sheets of card in various colours, including white and black
- scissors
- good quality glue stick

1 Choose one colour for your base; you will be gluing the rest of your shapes onto this card.

TIP!
Shape

When you cut out a shape, you actually have two pieces you can use for your artwork. The positive shape, which is the shape itself, and the negative shape, which is the area around and in between the shape. Use both pieces. Experiment with placing different coloured card under the cut-outs.

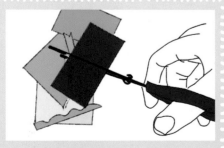

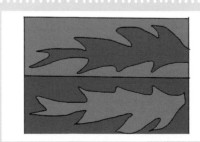

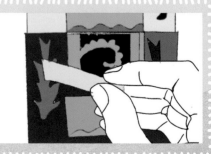

2 From the other coloured cards, cut irregular and geometric shapes.

3 Arrange the shapes on the base. Use both the positive and negative shapes. Try interlocking the pieces, overlapping them and creating some repetition.

4 Keep experimenting with the placement of the card shapes until you have a composition that you like.

Henri Matisse (1869–1954) was primarily known for being a painter and a leader in the Fauvism art movement, where artists used wild colours in unusual ways.

Following an illness that left him with limited mobility, Matisse began experimenting with shapes and patterns, and created a new art medium. For these cut-out artworks, he used a technique that he referred to as 'drawing with scissors'. To begin, Matisse asked his assistants to paint pieces of paper with gouache paint in various colours. When they were dry, he proceeded to cut out shapes with scissors from the painted sheets of paper. After all the pieces were cut, the process of arranging began, which involved pinning the pieces to his studio walls. Finally, the pieces were glued to a canvas or board. *Amphitrite* is a great example of this collage technique.

- What kinds of shapes do you see in *Amphitrite*? Amphitrite was an ancient Greek sea goddess so many of the shapes were inspired by sea plants.

- Matisse used colour in a way that made the shapes stand out, yet still created harmony. He often used bright complementary colours (see page 48) next to each other to great effect. What has he done here?

- Notice the layout: a grid-like structure with three rows and three columns.

- Notice the symmetry: the two halves mirror each other almost identically.

Composition
You may have to adjust the pieces to make them fit by cutting them, adding parts or even remaking some pieces.

You can choose a layout similar to the one Matisse used in *Amphitrite* or another one of his cut-outs, such as *La Gerbe* (1953) or *The Fall of Icarus* (1943), or discover your own!

5 When you're satisfied with your composition, carefully glue all the pieces. Make sure you keep some of the base colour showing.

TESSELLATION
WITH

Escher

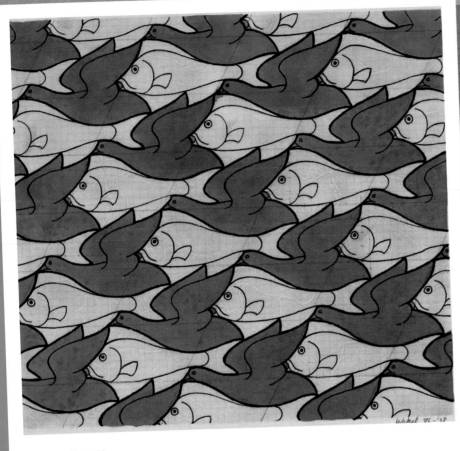

Fish, Bird (1938)

Dutch artist MC Escher (1898–1972) became fascinated with filling his artworks with eye-catching shapes and patterns. He briefly studied architecture before becoming a graphic artist. After visiting southern Italy, he found inspiration from the architecture he saw there, such as domed roofs.

Later, he saw beautiful Islamic tiling when he was visiting the Alhambra in Granada, Spain. Escher loved the order and the symmetry found in the decorative tiles arranged into repeating patterns. This led him to study mathematics, as well as the arrangement of space and pattern in tessellation. The artist added a fantastical element to the concept of tessellation to create eye-catching artworks such as *Fish, Bird*.

- Escher used two repeating, interlocking shapes in the image above: a fish and a duck. He arranged the shapes to form an interlocking repeating pattern.

- In this painting the use of just two colours brings out the repeating pattern.

MAKE A
TESSELLATION PICTURE

You will need

- white card
- 5 x 5 cm card for your stencil
- tape
- a ruler
- a pencil
- scissors (or cutting blade)
- acrylic paint
- two paintbrushes (one flat, one pointed)
- a medium-tip black marker pen

TIP!

Paintbrushes
Using two different sizes
and shapes of paintbrush
is helpful in this exercise:
a flat brush for the straight
edges and a small round
brush to get into the
tricky corners.

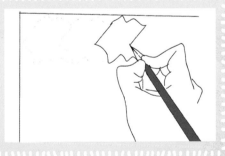

1 Use the 5 x 5 cm card to construct the
fish stencil by following the instructions
on page 56 or create your own shape.

2 Take the larger sheet of card, place the
stencil in one of the corners and trace
around it lightly with your pencil. Rotate the
stencil and interlock it into the first shape.
Try to make it fit, like a puzzle. Trace the
stencil. Keep doing this until your page is full.

3 Next, choose a monochromatic,
complementary or harmonious
colour scheme (see page 48).

4 Paint the shapes, alternating each
colour like the pattern on a chessboard.
Apply the paint in thin, even coats.

5 To finish, go over all your lines using
the medium-tip black marker pen.
Include the lines inside the fish shape to
create the fins, tail, eyes and mouth.

TEXTURE

Texture in art refers to how something feels, or how it looks like it feels. When we look at a surface, often we don't need to touch it to know its texture. When an artist has mastered the art of creating texture, it can be used to great effect.

MOOD AND DEPTH

From childhood, we explore the world through our sense of touch, which includes feeling the texture of objects (whether they are rough, smooth, hard or soft). Artists tap into our memories of the feel of objects (their texture), and how those textures made us feel emotionally, when they visually represent texture in their work.

Artists also use texture to create the illusion of depth in an artwork. The textures in the foreground will be larger and darker in tone than those in the background, as seen in Klimt's painting (right). He used oil paints and real gold to create this portrait.

Gustav Klimt (1862–1918) created the illusion of beautiful, original and decorative textures in his painting, *Portrait of Adele Bloch-Bauer I* (1907).

THREE-DIMENSIONAL ART

Three-dimensional artists, such as ceramic artists and sculptors, often use tools to create actual texture on the surface of their artwork. If you are allowed to touch the artwork, you will experience actual texture through your sense of touch, as opposed to visual texture, which is experienced through looking at the artwork.

Alberto Giacometti (1901–1966) created actual surface texture to produce a rough quality to his sculpture *Walking Man II (Detail)* (1960).

Pieter Claesz (1597–1660) used visual texture to create the illusion of bone, fabric, paper, wood and metal in this painting, *Vanitas Still Life* (1630).

ACTUAL AND VISUAL TEXTURE

In two-dimensional artworks, artists use line, tone and colour to create the illusion of texture but if you touched the artwork, it would be smooth to the touch. A visual texture is one that imitates the actual texture of an object for example, hard, soft, rough, smooth, furry or leathery. Finally, another type of texture is invented texture, which does not exist in nature: it is man-made, using the skills and imagination of the artist.

Ernst's TEXTURED LANDSCAPE

One day, dadaist and surrealist artist Max Ernst (1891–1976) was deep in thought when he noticed an interesting pattern and texture on his wooden floor. He wondered what would happen if he put a piece of paper on the floor and rubbed a pencil over the top. In this moment, he discovered a technique called frottage (French for rubbing) and he used it to create *Petrified Forest*.

- What objects did Ernst use to create the textures found in this artwork? Are they rough, smooth, jagged or furry?

- Notice Ernst's composition. He put the sun in the top centre. It looks like there is a river in the middle with tall trees on both sides. He used a low horizon line.

- Do you see the large 'M' in the artwork? Many have suggested that Max Ernst intentionally put his initial in each of his 'Forest and Sun' artworks. How could you insert a hidden symbol into your piece?

TIP!

Try holding the crayon flat to get a different result. Be sure not to get the wax crayon on the object, just on the paper. Like Ernst, you can try the floor, tree bark or whatever surfaces are available. Make sure you include a round object, like a disc.

EXPLORE TEXTURES

You will need
- found objects or materials with interesting textures
- six sheets of thin paper
- a pencil
- a dark-brown or black wax crayon

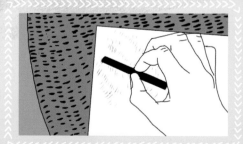

1 Trial the technique. Take a sheet of paper and the crayon and take a rubbing of an object or material that might create an interesting texture. Repeat with the other sheets of paper. Study all the different textures you've collected. Which ones will work the best for the landscape that you will create?

Petrified Forest, 1929

The areas in the background should be lighter in tone, creating a feeling of distance. The parts of the middle ground should be darker and the parts of the foreground should be the darkest. The rubbings will get darker the more layers you apply.

When designing a landscape, the objects in the background appear smaller then the objects in the foreground. You can overlap objects too, such as trees. This will create a sense of depth in your landscape (see page 37).

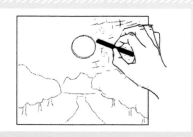

2 Try out your composition by completing two or more thumbnail sketches with a pencil. Start by drawing your horizon line.

3 Begin the artwork. On the paper, make a light pencil sketch of your composition.

4 Using your crayon, make a rubbing of your chosen material to fill in the background. Now fill in the middle ground. To achieve a slightly darker tone, press harder with the crayon. Now make rubbings to fill in the foreground. Press firmly on your crayon to get a dark tone.

Dürer's INVENTED BEAST

Look closely at this image of Albrecht Dürer's (1471–1528) famous *Rhinoceros* print. If you compare this print to a photo of a real Indian rhinoceros, you will find many differences. That is because Dürer had never seen a rhinoceros, as there were no rhinoceroses in Europe at the time. He created this image from a sketch and a written description. Dürer exaggerated many of the features, especially the textured armoured surface.

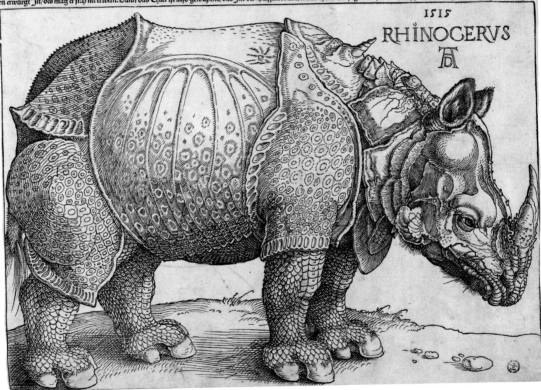

Rhinoceros (1515)

- How many different textures do you see? Notice the scale-like texture on its legs, which gives the impression of a very rough surface.

- See how Dürer created his textures. Some are created with simple hatch lines, others with circles.

- Notice where the darker tones are located on the rhinoceros. The light source is coming from above, shown by the highlighted areas, while darker tones create shadows under the rhino's body.

You will need

- a sheet of thin, smooth card
- 0.2 to 0.5 mm black technical pen
- a pencil
- your sketchbook
- a white rubber
- a black-and-white image of two of your favourite animals (print them the size that you will need for your final artwork)

Basic ink drawing techniques
When using pen and ink (see page 54), you need to begin by thinking about creating light, medium and dark tones. To make a lighter tone, place your marks far apart; to make a darker tone, place your marks closer together.

1 Decide what parts of which animal you want to use, such as the head of a tiger and the body of an owl. Next, draw all the animal parts using a pencil. Make as many modifications as you want to the animal. For example, add a horn on its back, as Dürer did, or different feet, eyes, a tail ... experiment!

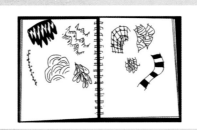

2 Texture exploration: in your sketchbook, create different textures. If you are unsure, look at Dürer's *Rhinoceros* for inspiration. Notice how the textures are created by repeating dots, lines and shapes.

3 Transfer your design onto your card with your pencil (see page 56). Make sure it is centred on the page. You could add a horizon line, as Dürer has.

Overlap and direction
When designing and placing your textures and patterns, consider the different parts of the animal that overlap. Using contrasting textures in these areas will help emphasise which areas are coming forwards and which are receding. Also consider the direction of the animal's fur or skin. Is it going left to right, or up and down? Apply the same direction to your textures.

4 Draw in the textures lightly with your pencil and then continue with the technical pen. When you have finished, rub out all your pencil lines.

TONE

Artists believe that understanding tone is important for all forms of art making. Tone is an element of art that refers to the different shades of light or dark. Artists build up tone to capture the way light falls on an object and how the light is reflected from its surface. Tone has a strong link to many of the other elements of art: line, texture, form and colour.

COMPOSITION

Tone is an important element in the development of the composition of an artwork (how you lay out your artwork). Many artists will complete a black-and-white thumbnail sketch, or tonal compositional study, of their subject to help compose their work in terms of shape, pattern and tone (shades of light and dark).

The use of contrasting tones is a great way of creating a focal point in a composition. In *Singer with a Glove*, Edgar Degas (1834–1917) used pastels to create contrasting tones (the dark tones of the glove and part of the background against the light tones of the face) to draw the viewer's eyes to the singer's pale face and gloved hand.

In Edgar Degas' pastel drawing, *Singer with a Glove* (1878), the use of black for the glove, the fur collar and part of the background emphasises the singer's pale face.

In *Ice Floes* (1893), Claude Monet's use of tone captures muted sunlight reflecting off chunks of ice and snow to create a muted, cold mood.

MOOD

Another way artists use tone is by choosing an overall tone to create mood or atmosphere in an artwork. There are three essential tonal value schemes. A low-key tonal value scheme is when most of the work is dominated by dark tones, which can provoke a dark, dramatic or sad mood. A high-key tonal value scheme uses the lightest tones creating a mood of calmness and playfulness. Finally a mid-key tonal value scheme represents a range of tones that can be seen at midday, creating transparency and simplicity in an artwork.

ILLUSION OF FORM

It is the gradual change from light to shadow that allows us to view form and perceive depth in the world around us. The same idea can be applied when creating the illusion of form within a two-dimensional artwork. An artist needs to use not only black and white to recreate an object, but also a range of grey tones. It is the tonal greys that give the illusion of form and reveal the most about an object and its relationship to its surroundings.

Artemisia Gentileschi (1593–1656) often used dramatic chiaroscuro, a strong contrast between dark and light tones, in her paintings. In *Self-Portrait as the Allegory of Painting* (1638–39), she mainly uses dark tones to contrast and emphasise her lit face.

31

Mondrian's GREY TREE

The Grey Tree (1911)

Piet Mondrian (1872–1944) was a Dutch abstract artist who is known for his use of black lines and limited colour schemes. Although this painting is generally linked with cubism, it is an important piece that shows his progression towards abstract art.

Mondrian uses expressive lines and brushstrokes to represent a tree. He only uses neutral colours – black, white and grey – but the different tones give the painting (a sense of) depth.

- The branches are made using curved, crooked and angular lines. They intersect and overlap; some are thick, others are thin.

- Notice the paint strokes in the background. They are mostly vertical or horizontal with some diagonal ones. This helps to create variety and movement.

PAINT A GREY TREE

You will need
- thick card or canvas
- a white pastel pencil
- white and black acrylic paint
- two flat paintbrushes (2.5 cm and 1 cm)
- a palette
- water
- a piece of cloth
- an image of your favourite tree

1 Paint a tonal strip (see below). Begin by painting the white and the black sections. Black will quickly overtake the white so add only a bit of black to the white to create your first tone of grey. Keep adding a very small amount of black to create the rest of the grey tones. Use this tonal strip as a guide, making sure that each tone is used in your drawing.

2 Next, paint a black background on your thick card or canvas. Leave it to dry.

3 Begin by using the white pastel to lightly draw the horizon line, and place the outline of the tree trunk slightly off centre. From the trunk, start drawing the outline of the larger branches. Continue by adding the smaller branches, until they reach the edges.

4 Prepare the acrylic paints (see page 54). Fill in the negative space, the areas between the branches, with a thin layer of mid-grey paint. Use short to medium brushstrokes. While the paint is still wet, add dark grey over the light, and light paint over the dark.

TIP!

Do your research
Although we all know what trees look like, have you ever really studied a tree? Notice the bends, twists and curves of the branches and the trunk. Study the way that famous artists, such as Vincent van Gogh, Gustav Klimt and Tom Thomson (1877–1917), have painted trees.

5 Add tiny, wispy branches using the small paintbrush. Try to follow the direction of the existing brushstrokes. Finally, add some texture to the trunk and larger branches. Keep the edges black and paint in a contrasting direction to the background paint strokes.

PRINTMAKING
WITH
Mary Cassatt

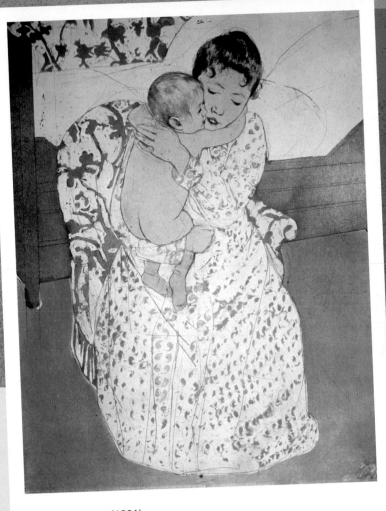

Maternal Caress (1891)

MAKE A
LINEAR MONOPRINT

You will need

- a black-and-white photograph of a person in action (playing/walking/running)
- a sheet of smooth, thin card
- a painting knife or spoon
- an ink roller
- masking tape
- a painting knife
- a stylus or technical pencil
- black Akua-intaglio printing ink
- a perspex sheet

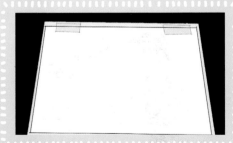

1 Study your photograph and try some thumbnail sketches to work out the composition – what details to leave in or out. The focal point in a portrait is the face, more specifically, the eyes. Complete a finished drawing that includes pattern, hatching or cross-hatching for variety, and adjust the tones to the design (see page 30) to create contrasting tones around the focal point.

2 In printmaking, the final image will be the mirror image of your drawing, so you need to make a reverse image for the print. You could turn over your card and retrace the lines on the back or you could scan your sketch and reverse the image with photo-editing software on a computer, and print it.

3 Transfer the reverse image onto the printing card (see page 56). Fix your card with masking tape to the perspex sheet.

Mary Cassatt (1844–1926) was an American painter and printmaker who was also part of the impressionist movement. *Maternal Caress* **is part of a series of skillful etching and drypoint prints that Cassatt produced later in her career.**

Etching is a printmaking technique where acid is used to cut lines into a printing plate, while drypoint is a printmaking process in which a design is drawn on a plate with a sharp point. Cassatt creates different tones using two different methods. Different shades (tones) of the same colour hue are used in the bed and the floor.

A variation in tone is also created by using different lines and patterns in the back wall, the chair and the mother's dress. To create tone using marks, it's important to remember that the further apart the marks are, the lighter the area will look. However, when marks are placed closer together, the area will appear darker.

- How many tones is Cassatt using in this print? Completing a tonal composition study (see page 61) is a great way to understand how an artist has created and emphasised the focal point using tone.

- Notice how Cassatt uses two very different patterns to influence tone and to add visual interest to her print. Consider adding pattern to change some of the tones in your artwork.

- See pages 28–29 and 54–55 to discover ways to create pattern and texture in an artwork.

 TIP!

Make a ghost print
After completing your print, place a new piece of card over the inked area. Using the back of a wooden spoon, press hard to rub over the entire paper area and lift the print.

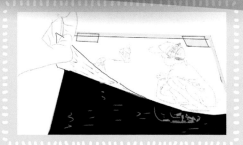

4 With a painting knife or a spoon, place a small amount of ink onto the perspex sheet. Using the roller, spread a thin layer to evenly cover the area under the card. Gently lay the card over the painted perspex sheet.

5 Without putting pressure on the card, trace the reverse drawing using the stylus. Use your other hand to steady and support your drawing hand. Work carefully but quickly or the ink will dry before you have finished.

6 As you are working, carefully lift the card to check your progress. When you have finished, remove the card and let it dry.

FORM

Although shape and form have much in common, and in everyday language we often substitute one term for the other, these two elements have different meanings in art. A shape is the area contained within a line and it is two dimensional, while form refers to a three-dimensional shape. A form has volume and occupies space: a circle becomes a sphere, a square becomes a cube and a triangle becomes a cone or a pyramid.

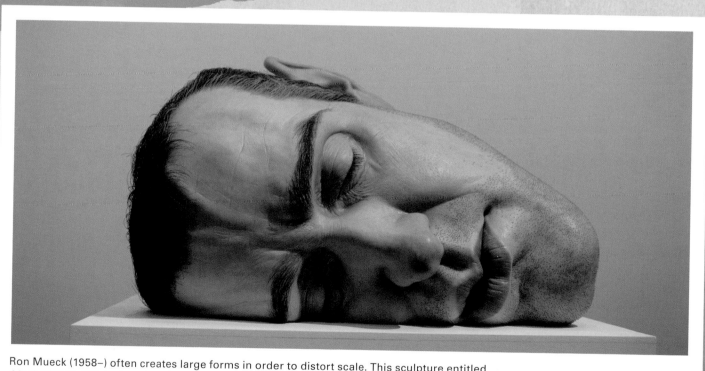

Ron Mueck (1958–) often creates large forms in order to distort scale. This sculpture entitled *Mask II* (2001–02), invites the viewer to take an intimate look at the artist's own face.

DIFFERENT DIMENSIONS

Like shape, forms can be either geometric or irregular (or free-form). Three-dimensional artists manipulate form in a real way; a ceramic artist can create a vessel that has volume and will take up actual space. Master sculptors manipulate both form and actual space in an intentional way to create works that have a physical impact on the viewer. An artist working on a two-dimensional surface must create the illusion that a form has volume and is taking up space.

Leonardo da Vinci was a master draughtsman who often used hatching and cross-hatching in his drawings to create form. In *Head of a Girl* (1483), da Vinci uses mostly hatch lines to give form to the face.

USING SHADING TO CREATE FORM

To create an illusion of form on a two-dimensional surface, it is important to understand both tone (the relative lightness and darkness of something) and perspective.

When using tone to produce an illusion of depth, an artist begins by focusing on the light source, and looks at the relationship between the highlights, shadows and the tones in between. Some of the drawing techniques used to create the illusion of form are stippling, hatching and cross-hatching, overlapping contour lines and tonal gradation. Colour can also be used to create the illusion of depth as the warm colours appear to come forwards while cool colours appear to recede.

USING LINEAR PERSPECTIVE TO CREATE FORM

Linear perspective, or perspective, uses converging lines within the composition to create the illusion of depth and volume. All the lines in the composition will recede towards a vanishing point, which is placed on a horizon line. Depending on the composition, an artist can use one, two or three vanishing points. This is called one-, two- or three-point perspective. Because an object occupies space, using perspective gives the impression that an object is receding into the distance.

In *House by the Railroad* (1925), American artist Edward Hopper (1882–1967) uses two-point perspective to recreate the three-dimensional form of an isolated and remote house.

DRAWING
Cézanne's APPLES

Still life with Seven Apples (1878)

Transforming a circle into a sphere, a three-dimensional form, is not difficult when you understand how tone works with form. An artist who painted a lot of spheres (well, apples) was artist Paul Cézanne (1839–1906).

In his painting *Still life with Seven Apples*, he has painted seven apples. A painting or drawing of objects that do not move is called a still life. Although still-life painting was not considered important by the impressionists, Cézanne loved the simplicity of forms found in nature, such as spheres, cylinders and cones. He used colour and tone to bring these apples to life.

- Can you work out where the light source is coming from? Hint: look at the lightest part of the apples and at the shadows they are casting.

- Notice how Cézanne uses seven apples. The rule of odds is when an artist uses an uneven number of objects in a composition. This is an important composition tip!

DRAW A
SPHERE

You will need

- two sheets of thin white card
- a ruler
- a 2H pencil
- willow charcoal
- compressed charcoal
- a putty rubber
- a chamois leather
- a blending stump (a tightly rolled up piece of paper)
- a spherical object such as a ball or an egg — make sure that the object is light coloured, as it will be easier to see the different tones
- a light source (a spotlight or desk lamp)

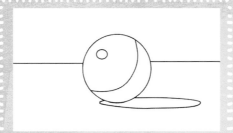

1 Begin by making a tonal scale (above). Draw six boxes using the ruler and 2H pencil. Shade an even layer of mid-grey with the willow charcoal in the last three boxes. Go over the sixth box with the compressed charcoal to make it black. Go over the fifth box to make the tone somewhere between the fourth and sixth boxes. And so on. Next, place your blending stump on the fourth box and drag it (and the charcoal) to the first box. Adjust each box by adding more charcoal, blending with the stump or rubbing out with the rubber.

2 Set up your still-life arrangement: put the spherical object on a piece of white paper, place your light source overhead and slightly to the left of the object to create ¾ lighting with strong shadows.

3 Lightly sketch the outline of the object and its shadow with your 2H pencil. Also, include the highlight and terminator line (the noticeable shadow line of the form shadow).

4 Begin by filling in the sphere's shadow area with an even, mid-grey tone. Use shading to fill in the rest of the shadow with slightly darker tones than the mid-grey but not black. Notice the reflected light on the bottom half of the sphere. Fill in the cast shadow with a dark tone but not black. See page 54 for tips on using charcoal.

5 Using your stump, while being mindful of tonal direction, smudge the charcoal towards the highlight. The tones get lighter as they get closer to the highlight. In the light areas, it can be difficult to achieve an even gradual tone. You may have to add some willow charcoal in the half-tone area of the sphere and continue blending with the stump.

6 Finally, add the dark accents using the compressed charcoal under the object and just below the top of the curved line that separates the light and dark areas under the sphere. You may need to rub out a little of the charcoal in the highlighted area. Keep practising! This is not as easy as it looks.

LINEAR PERSPECTIVE WITH *van Gogh*

An artist who often used linear perspective in his art was Vincent van Gogh (1853–1890). Depending on his subject matter, he would use one-point or two-point perspective.

In *The Bedroom* van Gogh uses one-point perspective to give the illusion of depth. The objects appear to be receding towards the back of the room. Van Gogh chose to challenge the rules of perspective by flattening certain areas, such as the chairs, the table and the back of the bed. This was one of van Gogh's favourite paintings. He wanted to create a feeling of comfort and tranquillity for himself and the viewer.

- Can you work out where the vanishing point is? Start by identifying the horizon line, which is eye level to the viewer. Notice where all the lines are converging.

- What colour scheme did van Gogh use to create this painting? It is important to note that the original colours have changed over the years and the walls were originally violet.

DRAW A ROOM

You will need
- a sheet of coloured pastel paper (use the smoother side)
- carbon paper
- a ruler
- 2H pencil
- paper towel
- a tortillon (blending tool)
- oil pastels
- a photo of a bedroom or hallway (make sure this is taken from the long, narrow end of the room, and not from a corner)

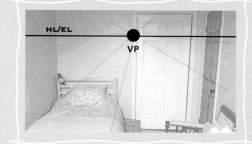

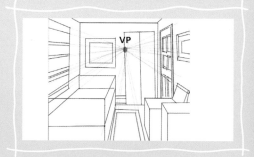

1 Begin by studying your photograph to discover the vanishing point (VP) and eye-level line. Mark these on your photograph. Consider what parts to remove, change or adjust.

2 Complete a sketch. Begin by placing the vanishing point and the back wall. Next, add the furniture by constructing simple forms, such as cubes and rectangular prisms, using one-point perspective. Continue to add the rest of the objects in the room or hall. Finally, add the details, while still considering perspective.

The Bedroom (1888)

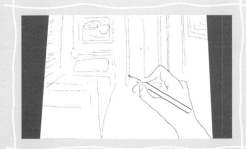

3 Transfer the image onto the pastel paper with a pencil using carbon paper (see page 56). Avoid using a ruler as this will give a more fluid quality to your lines similar to the ones found in van Gogh's painting.

4 Complete a few thumbnail sketches to help you decide on the colour scheme. Limit your palette to three colours, plus black and white.

5 Begin by completing the underpainting. Add a thin layer of pastel onto your paper, and blend with your fingers, or a paper towel. Next, begin building up the layers of pastel. It is a good idea to keep the pastels and your fingers clean while layering. If you make a mistake, you can scratch it out and add another layer over the top. See page 55 for more on pastels.

6 Finish by including small details with the edge of a pastel and a tortillon. Also, define any highlights with a tint or white.

SPACE

The element of space is one that can cause much confusion for both the artist and the student. Every day we use the word space in many different ways. We live in a world where we experience three-dimensional space, which is called actual space. We can refer to outer space, or to an inner space, like inside a house. Nowadays, we even have virtual space in computer games. Although there is some overlap when referring to space in art, there are many differences as well.

TWO AND THREE DIMENSIONS

Space can refer to the two-dimensional area of a picture plane – so the area of the canvas or paper. It can refer to the illusion of depth in a two-dimensional artwork. Space can also refer to the area above, below, beside and within the objects in both two-dimensional and three-dimensional artworks. A three-dimensional artist is manipulating the real space within and around an artwork. A two-dimensional artist is organising the illusion of space within the picture plane to create interesting compositions, while using many tools to create the illusion of depth.

In his large-scale sculpture, *Cloud Gate* (2006), artist Anish Kapoor (1954–), creates the form of a mirrored bean that not only changes the immediate space of Millennium Park in Chicago, USA, but distorts this city's skyline in its reflection.

POSITIVE AND NEGATIVE SPACE

In both two-dimensional and three-dimensional art, the primary objects or subjects are included as part of the positive space (figure), and its surroundings (which are not the main focus of the composition) are called the negative space (ground). An artist knows that the consideration of the weight of both the positive and negative spaces, which is called the figure/ground relationship, is essential for creating balanced compositions. Many artists will apply the golden ratio (see page 60) to the positive shapes to create dynamism and solidity.

Contemporary American artist, Kara Walker (1969–), is well-known for her unique and powerful works using silhouettes. In *Grub for Sharks, A Concession to the Negro Populace [detail]* (2004), (cut paper on wall, installation dimensions variable) her placement of these dark silhouettes on the stark white background not only plays with positive verses negative space, but also asks the viewers to consider racial issues and black history in the United States of America.

ILLUSION OF DEPTH

Two-dimensional artists will create the illusion of depth, or implied space, in an artwork, by using graduated tones and linear perspective (see pages 37 and 40–41). Linear perspective is a system for translating three-dimensional space into two dimensions. An artist will overlap objects, consider relative size and object placement, adjust the focus of details and consider atmospheric perspective (see page 60) to create the illusion of depth in an artwork. These principles are often used in landscape art.

In *Hunters in the Snow* (c 1565), Pieter Bruegel the Elder adjusts the size of the figures, overlaps objects, includes stronger details in the foreground and adjusts colour intensity to create the illusion of depth and space.

Giacometti's ELONGATED FIGURE

Walking Man II (1960)

Alberto Giacometti is known for his sculptures of elongated figures. He was an artist during and following the Second World War (1939–45) and these almost disintegrating figures express the feelings of sadness, loneliness and heaviness that were widespread following the war.

At a time when most artists were interested in abstract painting, Giacometti longed to bring the human figure back into mainstream art. A great example of this can be seen in this sculpture. It is about the height of an average man and has a very rough texture.

- Look carefully to see the negative space and shapes. Can you see the large triangle between the legs? What about the small triangle beside the arm?

- Notice the pose. The man is leaning forwards as he moves his weight from the back leg to the front leg. Although, this figure is stiff, it appears to be in mid-action, moving forwards.

 TIP!

The types of lines you will use to complete your quick gesture drawings in step 1 are the C-curve, the S-curve and the straight line. Most people start with the head. Notice the angle and tilt of the head. Next, draw a line of action, which is the first, fast, simple mark – or two – that conveys the direction and/or weight of the pose. It is a line that connects the head to the toes. Use these lines to show the arms, the body and the legs.

C-curve

S-curve

Straight line

DRAW AN
ELONGATED FIGURE

You will need

- sketching paper
- a graphite pencil
- white glue
- a sheet of black card
- chalk pastels

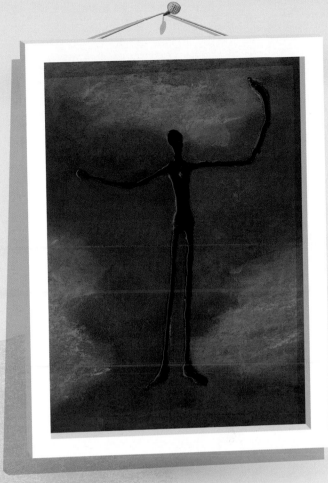

1 Ask a friend to pose for you so that you can complete a series of quick life-drawing sketches. Remember to elongate the figure like Giacometti, making the neck, legs and arms longer than usual.

2 Choose your best drawing and copy it onto black card with a pencil. Leave space below and above the figure. Next, fill in the shape with white glue. Leave to dry for six to eight hours.

3 Once dry, choose a harmonious colour scheme (see page 48). Begin by applying the first layer of pastels on your card. Rub it in with your finger or blending stump.

4 Apply a second layer of pastel and finally a third. The third layer should add brighter areas to your composition.

5 Clean the pastel dust that has built up on the dried glue to reveal your figure. You can use a fixative spray to prevent the chalk pastel from coming off the card.

STENCILLING WITH *Banksy*

Banksy (1975–) is a British street artist who prefers to remain unknown. Street art is created in public spaces, such as the walls of buildings, and is often considered to be vandalism, which is why Banksy uses a pseudonym. He uses graffiti to create art that addresses political and social issues.

His thought-provoking graffiti can be seen all around the world. *Leopard and Barcode*, thought to have been created around 1999–2000, is one of Banksy's earlier pieces. It shows a leopard breaking out of a cage formed from a barcode. There are many ways to interpret this piece, the most common being the illegal sale of wild animals. This is a great example of Banksy's use of an art technique known as stencilling.

Banksy used a stencil to create this artwork. Try to imagine what that stencil might have looked like. He cut out the areas that are black. It is important to have a good understanding of positive versus negative shape and space (see pages 20 and 44).

MAKE A
STENCIL PICTURE

1 Choose an animal on the endangered species list and print out a photo of it in black and white. Make sure the image shows the whole animal.

You will need

- a black-and-white photo of an animal on the endangered species list
- a black marker pen
- a pencil and paper
- two sheets of white card
- a cutting mat
- a cutting blade
- a small spray bottle
- acrylic paint or ink
- a newspaper

2 Trace the animal onto paper to try out your design. You will have to simplify the image by focusing on the contours. Remove all the smaller details.

Image!
Try to find an image that clearly shows the outline, the shapes and essential lines of your chosen animal.

3 This next part is tricky. Try to connect all the lines to make a series of closed shapes within your main outline. You now have an outline of the animal, with surface contour lines. Next, play with the thickness of the outline and surface contour lines: you will need to make these lines thicker in the shaded areas. Varying the weight of the line will help give your image variety and depth. You may need several attempts at the design.

Leopard and Barcode (2002)

TIP!

Colour
Use the natural colour of the animal or a more dramatic colour.
Choosing a darker hue (like blue instead of yellow) will create a more striking effect.

4 Make sure all the lines connect. Add in details such as eyes or other significant markings. It's important that these shapes link up with the contour lines you have already created.

5 Copy the lines onto card and very carefully cut out the negative space with a sharp blade and cutting mat.

6 Prepare your spray paint by putting some watered-down paint into the spray bottle. Test out the paint to get the right intensity. (Do this outside or in a large area with a lot of newspaper to protect the surface.) You can also use a sponging or dry brush technique to apply the paint. Use a sponge or a hard bristled paintbrush to gently dab, not brush, the paint onto the paper and stencil. Apply only thin layers of paint to avoid the paint bleeding outside the lines.

7 Overlay your stencil on another sheet of white card and start by spraying a light, even tone. You may want to add an additional layer, but avoid soaking the card as the paint will bleed under the stencil and create splodges. Carefully remove the stencil and allow the image to dry completely.

COLOUR

Often, when we look at a painting, it is the colours that first grab our attention. Colour can influence mood and emotions so an understanding of colour is essential to the artist. He or she can use this powerful element as a tool for creating art that will affect the viewer profoundly. Artists use the element of colour to reproduce objects, to create mood, to give the illusion of space and to direct the viewer's gaze within a picture.

THE COLOUR WHEEL

An important aspect of colour is the colour wheel (see page 11). The three primary colours are red, blue and yellow; they create all the other colours. When an artist blends two primary colours, he or she will produce a secondary colour, for example, mixing yellow and blue will produce green. By adjusting the ratios, an artist can achieve a variety of intermediate colours.

The colour wheel also reveals two other very important colour relationships: harmonious and complementary colours. Harmonious colours are the colours next to each other on the colour wheel, such as yellow, green and blue. These colours work well together to give a calming, peaceful effect. Complementary colours are two colours that are opposite each other on the colour wheel, such as blue and orange. When these colours are placed side by side, they create a vibrant effect. Together they stand out and create contrast.

Jan van Eyck (c. 1390–1441) cleverly uses red and green complementary colours to create a focal point in this painting, *Portrait of Giovanni Arnolfini and His Wife* (1434).

Although this painting, *Yellow City* (1914), is mostly made up of warm colours, Egon Schiele (1890–1918) dulls his colours to create a muted, less intense overall effect.

HUE, TONE AND INTENSITY

The colour wheel can also be divided into two parts: warm and cool colours. Warm colours are yellow, orange and red, while cool colour are blue, green and violet. Using this information, an artist is able to create different moods. For example, if an artist is creating a cold, winter scene he/she will use mostly cool colours. An artist can also use warm and cool colours to create the illusion of depth in an artwork as warm colours advance areas of the picture plane while cool colours recede into the background.

The use of colour can be overwhelming to an artist, as it is an element that can be somewhat difficult to understand and control. Colour possesses three properties: hue, tone and intensity. The hue is the name of the colour, such as blue, green or red. Tone, as seen on pages 30–31, describes the lightness or darkness of a colour. Finally, intensity describes the brightness or dullness of a colour. A colour becomes duller when its complementary colour is added to it, such as adding red to green.

Kandinsky's
COLOURFUL CIRCLES

Wassily Kandinsky (1866–1944), known as the founder of abstract art, was an artist who loved working with simple shapes and vibrant colours. He was also an art theorist, which means that he explored how theories of nature and its functions affected art. At the time, Kandinsky and many other artists were studying colour and its effect.

- Using the colour theory chart (see box), choose one block in Kandinsky's painting. Starting at the centre of the block, try to work out what effect Kandinsky was attempting to communicate.

- Notice how Kandinsky alternated contrasting colours and/or tones in each concentric circle. Sometimes the colours are blended and other times they are not.

Music played an important part in the development of his art. Kandinsky actually heard music when he painted colours, and saw colours when he listened to music. As he worked, he believed that he was making the colours in his paintings 'sing'. He wrote down his colour theory (see box) linking different colours to various emotions or moods.

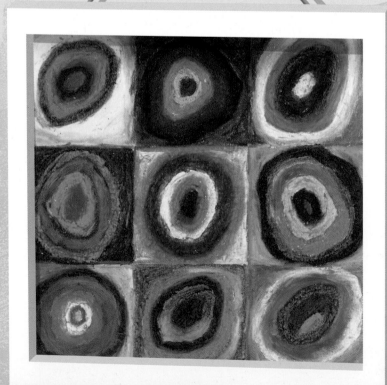

DESIGN A COLOUR CIRCLES PICTURE

You will need
- a 20 x 20 cm sheet of thick white card
- oil pastels (see page 55 for tips on testing pastels)
- a graphite pencil
- a ruler

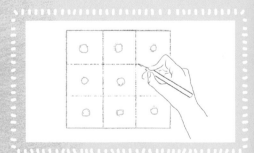

1 With your pencil and ruler, divide your card into nine squares.

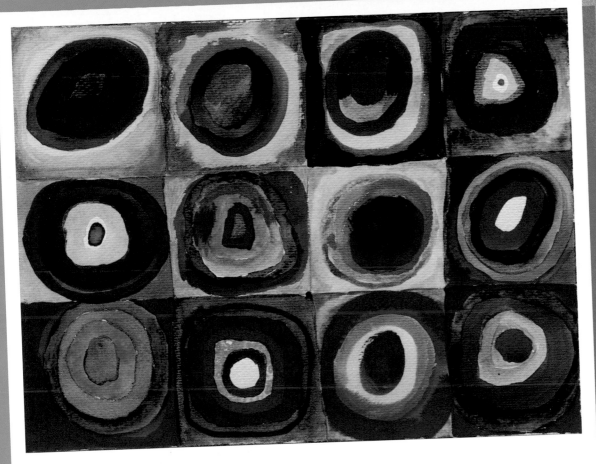

Squares with Concentric Circles (1913)

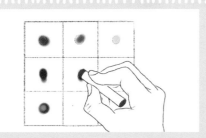

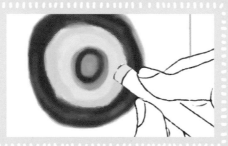

2 In the centre of each square, draw a different coloured circle, each about 1 cm in diameter.

4 Choose different colours and keep drawing more circles around the other circles, until they have reached the edge of the square.

TIP!

Colour!
Refer to the colour wheel (page 11) when blending colours. Try layering yellow over red or red over blue. Experiment: what happens when you mix two complementary colours?

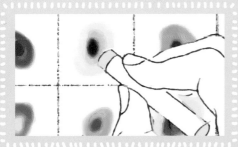

3 Circle each dot with a different colour. Experiment with how the different colours work with each other. Refer to the colour theory chart (right) to help you.

5 Colour in the remainder (edges) of the square until the section is filled with colour.

KANDINSKY'S COLOUR THEORY

Colour and its emotional effects captivated Kandinsky. Just as listening to music can affect mood and emotions, he believed that lines and colour in art affected emotions in the same way. Kandinsky began to use colour in a theoretical way, linking colour with specific emotions and sounds. The following is a brief version of Kandinsky's colour theory.

- Earthy, warm, madness
- Deep, peaceful, inner
- Stillness, peace, passive
- Hopeful
- Hopeless, immovable
- Strength, energy, joy
- Dull, hard, inhabited
- Radiant, healthy, serious
- Sad, morbid

A *Picasso*
COMPLEMENTARY COLLAGE

Collage is the technique of gluing bits of paper, images, words and/or found objects onto a paper or canvas. Although they did not invent this artistic technique, Pablo Picasso and Georges Braques (1882–1963) did name it by using the French word *coller* (to glue) to make collage very popular.

Many famous artists used collage to create striking images that convey emotions and social commentary. In this piece, Picasso assembled different bits of paper and added some details with paint in complementary colours. Can you see the fruit, the violin and the glass? The violin is composed of many different parts – different bits of paper and painted images. Picasso showed the violin from many different angles in one painting. This is called cubism.

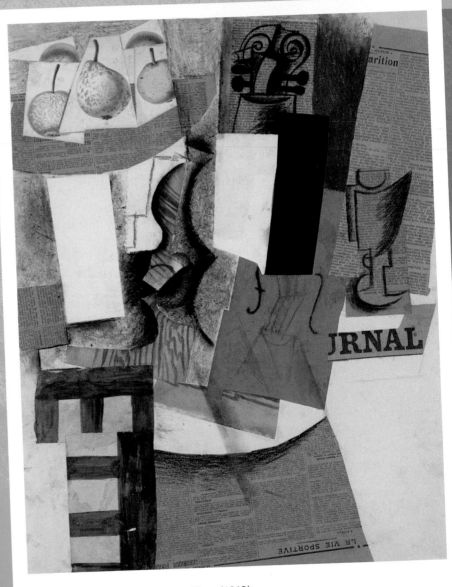

Compotier avec Fruit, Violon et Verre (1912)

- What colours are being used in this artwork? What area stands out?
  Using the blue to contrast with the orange helps to highlight the focal point.

- Notice the composition of this artwork. Did Picasso use the rule of thirds (see page 57) to place the focal point?

You will need

- a piece of paper or card (the colour of the card will be determined by your choice of the dominant colour)
- magazines or printed images
- scissors
- glue
- pens
- pencils
- a black oil pastel
- acrylic fluid medium

1 Choose complementary colours (example: blue and orange). Out of the two colours, choose one that will dominate your work and collect many images using that colour from magazines. Next, choose three images dominated by the contrasting colour. Add some black and white pieces too.

Plan

Plan and experiment with the significant object in step 5 before drawing on your collage. Choose an object and draw it from a variety of angles and in different sizes. Next, cut up your sketches and place them on your collage. Once you have found an effect that you like, draw it on your work.

2 Gather all your images of your dominant colour and start playing around with the arrangement, by overlaying, rotating and moving the pieces around. Consider the focal point. There are different types of compositions – see page 57 for some examples.

3 Once you've created an arrangement that you like, add the remaining three images in the contrasting colour.

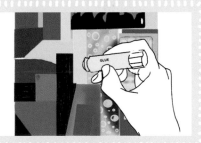

4 Glue all your pieces down. To give this a finished, refined look, put a thin layer of acrylic fluid medium over the work and let it dry.

5 Using a black oil pastel, you can draw in parts of a significant object such as a violin, a bottle or even a face. For inspiration, you could find one of Picasso's cubist portraits such as *Head of a Woman* (1960).

Exploring the medium

ACRYLIC PAINTING

(for the grey tree artwork, page 33)
Acrylic paint dries fast so it is important to work quickly. Test this wet-on-wet colour blending technique on a separate piece of card. Have the black, white and mid-grey paint ready on the palette. Begin by adding a small amount of water to your paint. Next, lay down a layer of mid-grey paint and apply each brushstroke in a slightly different direction. While the paint is still wet, add a little white onto the already loaded brush (so don't clean your brush) and apply it over the grey layers. Again, apply the paint in different directions. Try adding a little darker grey to your brush, and repeat the process. It is important not to over-blend the paint. Experiment until you achieve a result that you like.

EXPERIMENTING WITH CHARCOAL

(for the sphere, page 39)
Charcoal can be messy. A chamois leather helps pick up the unwanted powder. Working on a vertical surface such as an easel is advisable. Lay down layers of both types of charcoal as there are big differences between the two. Try blending with a stump, smudging the charcoal with the stump on the white paper, using your finger and layering the charcoals. Have fun experimenting!

BASIC INK DRAWING

(for the fantasy animal artwork, page 29)
These drawing techniques include hatching, cross-hatching, random lines and stippling. When using each of them, you need to begin by considering the tones in your artwork: light, mid and dark tones. To make a darker tone, you need to place your marks closer together and place them further apart for lighter tones (see top of page 55). Another way to accomplish a darker tone is to increase the width of the lines or dots, or to draw in an area.

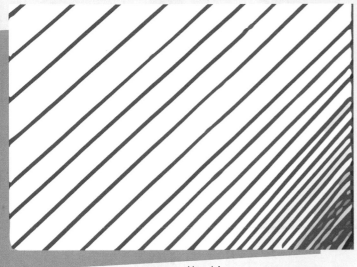

Hatching

Cross-hatching

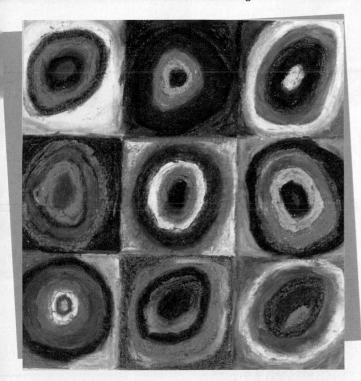

TESTING OIL PASTELS

(for the draw a room, page 40 and colourful circles picture, page 50)
Test an area of the work on a separate piece of card until you become used to oil pastels. They work best when they are a little soft, so warm them by holding them in your hands. It is important to keep your fingers and the pastel stick clean, so have a paper towel or cloth handy. Practise blending two colours with your fingertip and/or drawing one colour directly over another one. Try layering lighter hues over darker ones, and use black sparingly. Using a blade or knife, scratch lines out of the pastel, to create a *sgraffito* effect.

WATERCOLOUR PAINTING

(for the expressionist landscape, page 14)
Using watercolours can be tricky and difficult to control. Colours quickly mix together creating a bleeding effect, which is sometimes what you want, and sometimes not. Start by considering your lightest areas and work from light to dark. Keep in mind that your white areas will be the white of the paper. Try laying down a light wash of each colour. Allow each colour to dry before adding the next one. Next, try adding less diluted colour (more saturated) in some areas over your washes. It's best to test this medium and your colours on a separate piece of card and see what you prefer.

STENCIL-MAKING

(for the tessellation stencil, page 23) The process is the same whether you are making the fish for page 23 or inventing your own stencil. If you are creating your own shape, trace it on a separate piece of paper and try to 'see' a recognisable object in your shape. Perhaps you will discover that the shape looks like an exotic flower, a prickly tree or a strange bird. Be creative and have fun with it!

 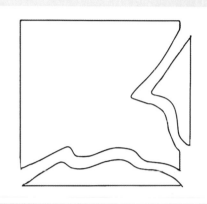 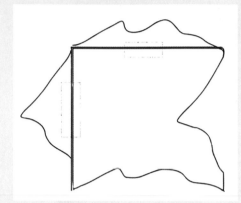

1 Draw along the edge of one or two sides of a 5 x 5 cm square card. You could try using a rectangular or triangular shaped card instead of a square piece.

2 Use scissors to cut out the shape.

3 Using tape, affix the cut pieces on the opposite side of the square card, making sure that the edges are correctly aligned.

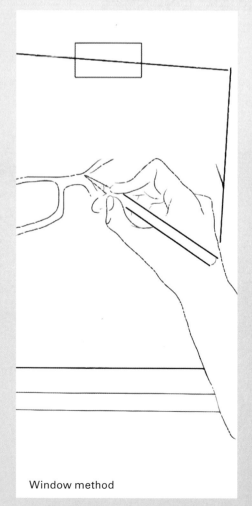

Window method

TRANSFERRING AN IMAGE

(for pages 29 and 34) Transferring an image or a drawing can be done in a number of ways.

Window method The simplest way to transfer an image onto card is to photocopy your desired image onto plain paper. Tape this image onto a bright sunny window. Next, place your card over the photocopied image and trace. Or you could use a tracing lightbox, which works in a same way.

Graphite transfer If you are using a canvas for your artwork, graphite transfer or projecting your image will work best. There's an easy way to make your own graphite transfer. On the back of the sheet of your drawing or photocopy, apply an even layer of graphite using a 6B or 8B graphite pencil. Next, place your canvas under the sheet and trace your image using a 2H pencil or a biro. If you don't wish to make your own paper you can use carbon paper, available from stationers, to transfer images. Follow the instructions that come in the pack.

Grid method If you need to enlarge your image, you could use either a projector or the grid method. For the grid method, you will need a ruler, a paper copy of your reference image and a pencil. First begin by drawing a grid over your reference image. Next, draw a grid of equal proportions on your large surface or canvas. Begin drawing the overall outline, then draw the outline of the large shapes and finish by adding the details. Finally, rub out all the grid lines.

Art rules AND tools

THE RULE OF THIRDS

The picture plane can be divided into nine equal parts. Your focal point or main subject should be placed on, or very near, to one of the connection points. Your horizon line should be placed on, or very near, to one of the horizontal lines to create a high horizon line or a low horizon line. A horizon line is a horizontal line that crosses the picture plane at eye level to the artist (and viewer).

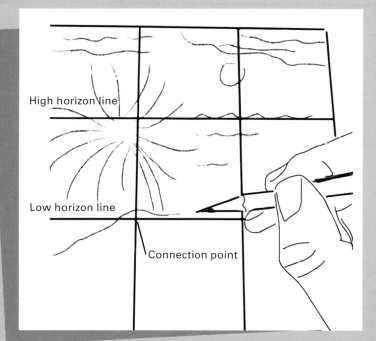

LINEAR PERSPECTIVE

Also called pictorial depth or just perspective, linear perspective is an important tool that artists have used over many centuries to create the illusion of form and depth in an artwork. The artist will use one-, two- or three-point perspective, meaning that the image has one, two or three vanishing points on the horizon line. All the lines in the picture plane will converge on the vanishing points.

One-point perspective (where VP is the vanishing point).

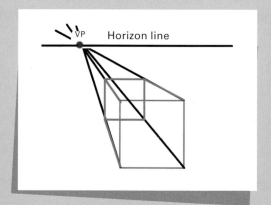

FIVE COMMON COMPOSITIONS

Each of these compositions can be altered in direction and/or angle to fit any format. Keep in mind the focal point and the rule of thirds.

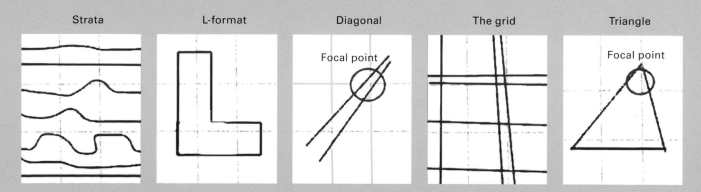

Strata   L-format   Diagonal   The grid   Triangle

Art movements

ABSTRACT ART

The word abstract means to separate or remove something from something else. Abstract art does not try to represent something accurately or realistically. In the early 20th century, some artists wanted to remove all the unnecessary parts of a subject to reveal its true essence. They began to simplify their subjects into basic shapes, lines and colour to emphasise form instead of accurate or representational depictions. The subjects can be either a figure, a landscape, an object, or may not depict anything in the natural world. Some art movements that were influenced by abstract art are: surrealism, dadaism, cubism and Fauvism.

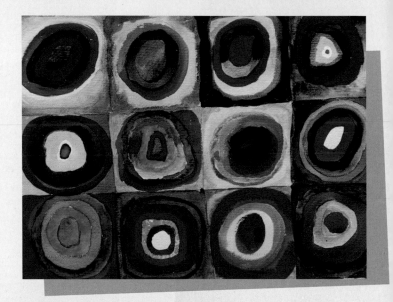

CUBISM (1907-1914)

The works of Pablo Picasso and Georges Braque are generally seen to be significant in the development of cubism, one of the most important art movement of the 20th century, which started with *Les Demoiselles d'Avignon* by Picasso in 1907. In their work, cubist artists attempt to show different viewpoints of a figure or an object at the same time, within a limited space. Objects are dissected, depicted at different angles and reassembled in one artwork.

DADAISM (1916-1920)

Dada or dadaism emerged during the early twentieth century, a time of great political turmoil. A group of artists, reacting to what was happening around them, rejected conventional ideas about art and created works of art that were often experimental, controversial, even nonsensical.

EXPRESSIONISM

The term expressionist refers to art created mostly in the 20th century and is often said to have begun with the work of van Gogh. The expressionists' aim was to depict what they felt about the world rather than how it looked, choosing to express their feelings and emotions in their artworks. These artists put aside traditional art techniques and teachings in order to further the expressive quality of their work. Many of them, such as Edvard Munch, Paul Klee and Wassily Kandinsky, used intense colours, exaggerated forms and applied expressive brushwork to create their masterpieces.

FAUVISM (1905-1910)

Fauvism is the word used for the work of a group of artists known as *les fauves*, French for 'the wild beasts', between 1905 and 1910. The artists simplified form, used bold, obvious brushstrokes and vibrant colours. Key artists include Henri Matisse, André Derain and Maurice de Vlaminck.

IMPRESSIONISM (1867-1886)

French artists including Claude Monet, Paul Cézanne and Edgar Degas were the first to present this style of painting in an exhibition they held in Paris, France in 1874. Monet's painting, *Impression, Sunrise* (1874), gave its name to this important art movement. Impressionist artists painted outside, *en plein air*, and used unusual angles in their compositions to capture everyday life and scenes from nature. The paintings featured short brushstrokes and a brighter colour palette. They were not trying to make realistic depictions of their subjects but rather capture an impression of it, focusing on light and its effect on colour.

MODERN ART (1860-1960)

The term modern art is usually used to describe the succession of art movements that developed from the mid 19th century onwards, when artists began to break away from traditional, classical art and its beliefs. Instead of focusing on realistic depictions of subjects, artists experimented with shape, colour and line, often using abstraction as well as experimenting with materials and techniques to express the new ideas of a modern society. Some of the key art movements in modern art are: impressionism, cubism and surrealism.

NEO-IMPRESSIONISM (1886-1906)

Neo-impressionism is an art movement founded in France by George Seurat. It differs from impressionism as the artist focused more on optical theory and painted using tiny dabs of primary colour to create the effect of light. The artists believed this technique would create a shimmering effect of light and stronger colour vibrancy. The technique came to be known as pointillism or divisionism.

POP ART (1950-1960)

Pop artists chose to represent popular images from the media and advertising in their artwork, elevating the everyday image to art. Although pop art began in Britain, it quickly became known as an American art movement with artists such as Andy Warhol, Roy Lichtenstein and James Rosenquist.

STREET ART (GRAFFITI ART) (1980-PRESENT)

Street art is linked to graffiti, which is writing or drawings that have been scribbled, scratched or painted on public property. Graffiti began as social and political commentary on public walls in the 1960s and 1970s. From the 1980s, graffiti became very popular with artists such as Keith Haring, changing graffiti into the subversive art form known as street art. Street art remains for the most part illegal, and some maintain that this is a vital aspect of the form. Ironically, street art is now being sold to art collectors and galleries.

SURREALISM (1920-1930)

The art movement where dreams, imagination and the subconscious mind served as inspiration for artists such as Salvador Dali and Max Ernst. There are two main types of surrealism: dream-like imagery and automatism. Artists often used free association and automatism to access the subconscious mind. Automatism is where artists allow their hand to randomly move across the paper, like doodling, guided by their subconscious mind in order to reveal repressed feelings and desires.

Glossary

A

ABSTRACT See Abstract art (page 58).

ACRYLIC A synthetic, quick-drying paint that can be used in thick, heavy layers or thin washes on most surfaces.

ACRYLIC FLUID MEDIUM Used in acrylic painting to thin the paint, and increase or decrease gloss.

APERTURE The opening that controls the amount of light that reaches a camera's sensor. The larger the aperture, the more light reaches the sensor.

ATMOSPHERIC (OR AERIAL) PERSPECTIVE The art technique of showing more distant objects as fainter and more blue.

B

BACKGROUND This is the area in the back of the picture plane that appears furthest from the viewer. In a landscape, it is often at the top of the image. In this area of the landscape, the objects will be smaller, the details are not visible and it often has a bluish tinge, which is called atmospheric perspective (see above).

BALANCE A principle of art that refers to how the elements are arranged in an artwork. There are three types of balance: symmetrical, asymmetrical or radial.

BEN-DAY DOTS A printing process invented by printer and illustrator Benjamin Henry Day Jr. in 1879. Small coloured dots are closely-spaced, widely-spaced or overlapped.

BLEEDING When a colour unintentionally spreads to another area of the painting where it is not wanted or when a dark colour 'bleeds' or spreads into a lighter colour. Bleed is also a term from printing when the image extends beyond the trim edge, leaving no white margin.

BLENDING STUMP (TORTILLON) A cylindrical blending tool used to smudge or blend charcoal, pastels, etc.

C

CAST SHADOW The shadow that is cast by the object. The cast shadow may fall on surrounding objects and surfaces.

CHARCOAL A black porous form of carbon produced by heating wood in little or no air. Artists use sticks of charcoal for drawing.

COLOUR BALANCE Related to balance, one of principles of art and design; one way that colour balance is achieved is by using similar colours, in small amounts, throughout the artwork.

COLOUR SCHEME A planned arrangement of colours to be used in an artwork. For example, a colour scheme may be warm or cool, and/or consist of complementary or harmonious colours.

COLOUR THEORY A system of ideas constructed to understand colour and its relationships and effects.

COMIC ILLUSTRATION A semi-realistic drawing or painting that often shows humour or satire.

COMPLEMENTARY COLOUR Two colours that are opposite each other on the colour wheel. Used to create a strong colour contrast.

COMPOSITION The arrangement of all the visual elements or ingredients in a work of art.

CONTOUR A line that shows the edges and surface edges of an object.

CONTRAST This is a principle of art that is achieved by arranging opposite elements to create a focal point in an artwork. Example: contrasting colour, shapes or lines.

CRITIQUE A detailed analysis and assessment of a work of art.

CROSS-HATCHING A shading technique where an artist makes lines cross each other.

CUBISM See page 58.

D

DADAISM See page 58.

DARK ACCENT The area of the shadow that are black, usually under the object.

DEPTH The illusion of space, distance or three-dimensions. Perspective and overlap are two ways to create depth in works of art. See Background and Foreground.

DESIGN A plan or organisation of the elements of art in the artwork.

DRY BRUSH A technique of drawing or painting in which a hard-bristled brush with a small quantity of pigment is applied to, or dragged across, a surface.

E

ELONGATED Creating an image or figure of the human body, where the length of various parts of the figure are longer than they are in reality.

ETCHING Picture made by putting ink on an etched (or engraved) piece of metal and then pressing paper against the metal plate.

EXPRESSIONISM See page 58.

F

FAUVISM See page 58.

FIGURE The human form in a work of art. Figurative art describes any form of modern art that retains strong references to the real world and particularly to the human figure. Also, Figure refers to the positive space in the figure/ground relationship (see page 42).

FIGURE DRAWING The pictorial study or representation of the human body.

FOCAL POINT The centre of interest of an artwork.

FOREGROUND The area of the picture plane that appears closest to the viewer. In this part, the details will be clear, the colours will be more intense, the objects will be larger in size and they are often at the bottom of the picture plane.

FORM An element of art that is three dimensional (height, width and depth) and encloses volume.

FORM SHADOW The shadow that is on the object.

FROTTAGE A technique to create a textural effect or image by rubbing pencil, charcoal, etc, over paper laid on a textured surface.

G

GEOMETRIC SHAPE Regular shapes made out of points and lines, such as circles, squares and triangles.

GESTURE DRAWING A quick drawing that captures the essential form of a subject.

GHOST PRINT A second print from the original plate is called a 'ghost print'.

GOLDEN RATIO Also called the golden mean, this is a proportional ratio (1:1.618) that has been used by many great artists, especially Leonardo da Vinci, to achieve beauty and balance in the design of an artwork.

GRAFFITI See Street art (page 59).

H

HALF-TONE (Middle-tone) The half-tones are part of the illuminated side of an object neither In the highlight or in the form shadow.

HARMONIOUS COLOURS (Also known as analogous) Colours that are next to each other on the colour wheel. They are often found in nature and pleasing to the eye.

HATCHING A shading technique that includes a series of fine parallel lines. These lines can be straight or curved.

HIGHLIGHT The little area of white light that is being reflected from your light source.

HORIZON LINE This is a horizontal line that crosses the picture plane. It is at eye level to the viewer and is used to create perspective. Often, it is shown where the land meets the sky.

HUE The first property of colour. It is the name of a colour, for example red, blue, yellow.

I

ILLUSION In art, depicting something so realistically that it appears to be real and have form (three dimensions).

IMPRESSIONISM See page 59.

IMPLIED LINES Lines that aren't necessarily there but which our eyes 'see', as a result of an artist's skilled use of tone, colour, texture etc.

INTENSITY One of the three properties of colour. It refers to the brightness or dullness of a colour.

IRREGULAR SHAPE (also called organic or free-form shapes) A shape that is not geometric. They are often found in the natural environment and in living things.

ISLAMIC ART Relating to motifs, architecture and patterns that was created by or influenced by Muslim cultures. Because of religious beliefs, Islamic art focuses primarily on depictions of complex repetitions of shapes, lines and colours.

L

LANDSCAPE The depiction of a natural area in an artwork, such as mountains, trees and lakes, as the main subject matter.

LIFE DRAWING The act of drawing the human figure from a living model generally without clothing.

LIGHT DRAWING or light painting. A photographic technique that uses long exposure in dark surroundings and a moving light source.

LIGHT SOURCE The direction from which the main light is coming. Its placement shows where to draw the light, mid-tones and the shadows.

LINEAR PERSPECTIVE A form of perspective in drawing and painting in which lines are represented as converging so as to give the illusion of depth and distance.

M

MEDIUM: The material that artists use to create their art, for example oil paint on canvas or wood.

MIDDLE GROUND The area located between the background and the foreground in a painting or drawing. This is often where the main action takes place.

MONOCHROMATIC A colour scheme that uses only one colour in different tints or shades.

MONOPRINT A form of printmaking where an image can be made only once.

MOVEMENT Movement is a principle of art and design. Movement is the suggestion of motion in a work of art, either by showing a gesture in a painting or sculpture, or by the relationship or repetition of the elements in a composition.

N

NEGATIVE SPACE Empty spaces surrounding forms or shapes. Negative space greatly affects how the positive spaces (the subject) are interpreted.

NEUTRAL COLOURS Black, white and grey. The colours are not associated with a specific hue. Often brown and beige are considered neutral colours.

O

OUTLINE A line that shows the outer edge of a shape.

OVERLAP In art, the placement of two objects one over the other to create the illusion of depth; the object in the back appears to be receding, while the object in the front appears to be coming forwards, towards the viewer.

P

PATTERN A principle of art that consists of repeating elements, such as lines, shapes and texture, to create a design.

PEN AND INK A technique of drawing using ink pens, or ink and dip pen, or ink and brush.

PERSPECTIVE See also Linear perspective. The technique used by artists to create the illusion of three-dimensional space on a two-dimensional flat picture surface (paper, canvas, wood). Objects in the background appear smaller than those in the foreground.

PICTURE PLANE The picture plane is the flat surface on which the artwork (painting, drawing etc) is created. The illusion of three dimensional images is created on the picture plane.

POINTILLISM See page 59.

POP ART See page 59.

PORTRAIT A likeness of a person, especially of the face, as a painting, sculpture, drawing or photograph.

POST-IMPRESSIONISM See page 59.

PREDOMINANT COLOUR The main colour in an artwork.

PRIMARY COLOURS Red, yellow and blue. These three colours are used to create all the other colours.

PRINTMAKING The design and production of prints by an artist.

PROFILE An outline of the face, or side view of the head.

PROPORTION A principle of art that describes the size, location or amount of one element to another (or to the whole) in a work.

R

REFLECTIVE LIGHT An area of the artwork where the light is reflected from other surrounding objects and surfaces.

RENAISSANCE The rediscovery and revival of interest in the arts of classical Greece from the 14th–16th centuries in western Europe.

RULE OF ODDS When an artist uses an uneven number of objects in a composition.

S

SATURATED The intensity of colour in an image.

SCALE The size of the object. In experiencing the scale of an artwork we tend to compare its size to the size of our own bodies.

SHADE Any hue with black added to it.

SHAPE An enclosed, two-dimensional space, which can be irregular, geometric, abstract or symbolic.

SHUTTER SPEED How long the camera shutter is open (or how long the sensor is exposed to light), creating a freezing action or blurring motion on the photo.

SHUTTER SPEED PRIORITY A shooting mode on your camera, where the camera will automatically adjust the aperture depending on how long the shutter is open.

SPACE An element of art that refers to the area between, within and around the objects in the picture plane (see pages 42–43).

STENCIL A cut-out where a shape or pattern is cut out of a piece of cardboard, plastic or metal. Paint, ink and a variety of other media can be used to fill the cut-out area to produce a copy of the cut design.

STENCILLING A printing technique that involves using a cut-out of a shape. A stencil is often constructed out of thick card or plastic.

STILL LIFE A painting, drawing or photo of a carefully arranged group of inanimate objects, such as flowers and fruit.

STIPPLING A technique of shading using dots.

STREET ART See page 59.

SYMMETRY Related to the art principle balance, where two halves of a composition are practically identical.

SURREALISM See page 59.

T

TERMINATOR The line on the object that separates the light values and the dark values. Sometimes this line can be seen clearly, but depending on the lighting, it can be blurred, a broken line, or a combination of these

TESSELLATION A tessellation is created when a shape is repeated over and over again covering a surface without any gaps or overlaps. Another word for a tessellation is tiling.

TEXTURE The surface quality of a work of art, which can be actual or visual. **Actual texture** A surface that may be experienced through the sense of touch. **Visual texture** The copying, or imitation, of actual object surfaces.

THEME A general idea or message conveyed in the work of art.

3/4 LIGHTING Lighting where three quarters (or two thirds) of the object is lit.

THUMBNAIL SKETCH A small, exploratory drawing used to try out various ideas for an artwork or project. Also used to study tones or to plan the composition of an artwork.

TINT Any hue (colour) with white added to it, to make it lighter.

TONAL COMPOSITION STUDY The study and observation of the arrangement of shapes and their tone in an artwork. By breaking down the image into simple shapes determined by tone, it becomes easier to observe the balance of tone.

TONAL DIRECTION When shading, following the direction or the curve and contours of the object to express the illusion of volume.

TONAL SCALE A sequence of tones from light (white) to dark (black) of one particular hue.

TONE (Also known as value) Referring to the relative lightness or darkness of something and the visual representation of this in an artwork. It can also refer to the lightness or darkness of a colour.

TONAL DIRECTION When shading follows the direction or the curve of the object.

U

UNDERPAINTING The first coat of paint, especially the initial painting on a canvas (or surface) in which the major areas, tones, colours and forms are shown.

V

VANISHING POINT A point at which receding parallel lines seem to meet creating a sense of form and depth in the artwork.

VARIETY A principle of art that refers to ways of combining art elements in involved ways to achieve intricate and complex relationships.

VISUAL TEXTURE When the surface of a painted (or drawn) object looks real.

W

WATERCOLOUR A paint made from a binding material (such as glue or gum) and water.

WOODCUT Making a 'stamp' by carving out images in a block of wood.

Index

FURTHER READING

Inspiring Artists series by Various (Franklin Watts)

The Usborne Book of Famous Artists by Various (Usborne)

13 Artists Children Should Know by Angela Wenzel (Prestel)

Picture acknowlegements

Art Institute of Chicago. Wikimedia Commons: front cover, 1r, 6bl, 11t.

Banky, © the artist. Private Collection: 47.

© The Estate of Jean-Michel Basquiat/ADAGP, Paris and DACS, London 2017: 18.

Biblioteca Reale, Turin.Hulton Archive/ Getty Images: 37t.

Sonia Delaunay. © Pracusa 2014083. Javier Larrea/age fotostock/Superstock: 19.

ESB Basic/Shutterstock: 11b.

M.C. Escher's "Symmetry Drawing E22" © _2017 The M.C. Escher Company-The Netherlands. All rights reserved. www.mcescher.com: 22.

© The Estate of Alberto Giacometti (Fondation Giacometti, Paris and ADAGP, Paris), licensed in the UK by ACS and DACS, London 2017: 25t, 44.

Fogg Museum, Harvard Art Museums, Cambridge, MA. Bridgeman Images: 30.

Gemeentemuseum, Den Haag, Jan Fritz/Superstock: 32.

© Estate of Edward Hopper, orphan work. Museum of Modern Art, New York/ Bridgeman Images: 37b.

© Anish Kapoor. All Rights Reserved, DACS, London 2017: 42.

Kunsthistorisches Museum, Vienna: 43b.

Lenbachhaus, Munich/AKG: back cover, 51, 58.

© Estate of Roy Lichtenstein/DACS, London 2017: 6cr, 8, 59.

Archives H. Matisse. © Succession H. Matisse/ DACS, London 2017: 20.

Mauritshaus, Den Haag: 25b.

© The Henry Moore Foundation, 2017. Crown copyright. Photo © Tate, Creative Commons CC-BY-NC-ND: 12cr.

© the artist Ron Mueck. Hauser & Wirth, London. Tiago Mazza Chiaravalloti/ NurPhoto/Getty Images: 36.

Musée d'Art Moderne, Centre Pompidou, Paris.© The Estate of Max Ernst. ADAGP, Paris and DACS, London 2017. Bridgeman Images: 27t.

National Gallery of Art, Washington. Superstock: 34.

National Gallery of Art, Washington. Wikimedia Commons: 28.

National Gallery, London. Bridgeman Images: 48.

National Gallery Oslo/Bridgeman Images: 13.

Neue Gallery, New York/Superstock: 24.

Philadelphia Museum of Art, PA. Gift of Mrs. Frank Graham Thomson, 1961: 31t.

Philadelphia Museum of Art, PA. © Succession Picasso/DACS, London 2017: 52.

© Succession Picasso/DACS, London 2017. Gjon Mili/The Life Picture Collection/ Getty Images: 16.

Pollock-Krasner Foundation. © ARS, NY and DACS, London 2017: 12bl.

Private Collection: 15.

Private Collection. Imagno/Artothek: 49.

The Royal Collection, London. Fine Art Images/Superstock: 31b.

Van Gogh Museum, Amsterdam. Getty Images: 41.

Vladvm/Shutterstock: front cover tl, br, 1l.

© the artist Yayoi Kusama. All rights reserved. Photo Simon Falvo: 7.

Artwork © Kara Walker, courtesy of Sikkema Jenkins & Co, New York: 43t.

Zenodot Verlagsgesellschaft mbH, GNU Free Documentation License. Wikimedia Commons: 38.

Every attempt has been made to clear copyright. Should there be any inadvertent omission please apply to the publisher for rectification.